DARE TO DISCIPLINE
BIBLE STUDY
ANSWERS TO YOUR TOUGHEST PARENTING QUESTIONS

DR. JAMES DOBSON

developed with Nic Allen

LifeWay Press®
Nashville, Tennessee

Published by LifeWay Press®
© 2014 Siggie, LLC

The New Dare to Discipline © 2014 by Dr. James Dobson. Published by Tyndale House Publishers;
Carol Stream, IL. Used by Permission.

ISBN: 978-1-4300-3295-3
Item: 005650369

Dewey decimal classification: 649
Subject headings: CHILD REARING \ CHILD DEVELOPMENT \ PARENT-CHILD RELATIONSHIP

All Scripture quotations are taken from the Holman Christian Standard Bible. Copyright © 1999,
2000, 2002, 2003, 2009 by Holman Bible Publishers. Used by permission. Holman Christian Standard
Bible® and HCSB® are federally registered trademarks of Holman Bible Publishers. Cover photo: Thinkstock

To order additional copies of this resource, write to LifeWay Church Resources, Customer Service,
One LifeWay Plaza, Nashville, TN 37234-0113; fax 615.251.5933; phone 800.458.2772; order online
at *www.lifeway.com* or email *orderentry@lifeway.com;* or visit the LifeWay Christian Store serving you.

Printed in the United States of America.

Adult Ministry Publishing, LifeWay Church Resources, One LifeWay Plaza, Nashville, TN 37234-0152

Contents

Author Page

DR. JAMES DOBSON is the founder and president of Family Talk, a non-profit organization that produces his radio program, "Dr. James Dobson's Family Talk." He is the author of more than 50 books dedicated to the preservation of the family, including *The New Dare to Discipline; Love for a Lifetime; Life on the Edge; Love Must Be Tough; The New Strong-Willed Child; When God Doesn't Make Sense; Bringing Up Boys; Bringing Up Girls; Head Over Heels;* and, most recently, *Dr. Dobson's Handbook of Family Advice.*

Dr. Dobson served as an associate clinical professor of pediatrics at the University of Southern California School of Medicine for fourteen years and on the attending staff of Children's Hospital of Los Angeles for seventeen years in the divisions of Child Development and Medical Genetics. He has been active in governmental affairs and has advised three U.S. presidents on family matters.

He earned his PhD from the University of Southern California (1967) in child development and holds eighteen honorary doctoral degrees. He was inducted in 2009 into the National Radio Hall of Fame.

Dr. Dobson and his wife, Shirley, reside in Colorado Springs, Colorado. They have two grown children, Danae and Ryan, and two grandchildren.

NIC ALLEN helped with the curriculum development of this study. After spending ten years in student ministry, Nic became the family and children's pastor at Rolling Hills Community Church in Franklin, Tennessee. Nic has written for several LifeWay Bible studies, including *Courageous, Facing the Giants,* and *Flywheel.* Nic and his wife, Susan, have three children: Lillie Cate, Nora Blake, and Simon.

How to Use This Study

The four sessions of this study may be used weekly or during a weekend retreat. But we recommend that before you dig into this material, you watch the film, *Dare to Discipline* from the *Dr. James Dobson Presents: Building a Family Legacy* film series. This will lay the groundwork for your study.

This material has been written for a small-group experience, for you and your spouse, or for personal study.

An option to extend or conclude this study is for your group to view the film *Your Legacy* from the *Dr. James Dobson Presents: Building a Family Legacy* film series.

CONNECT: The purpose of the introductory section of each session invites and motivates you to connect with the topic of the session and others in your group.

WATCH: The study DVD contains four DVD clips which include introductions from Ryan Dobson and clips from a talk by Dr. James Dobson, based on the film and the accompanying book *The New Dare to Discipline* by Dr. Dobson (Tyndale Momentum; ISBN 978-1-4143-9135-9.)

ENGAGE: This section is the primary focus of each week's group time. You and the other participants will further engage the truths of Scripture and discuss accompanying questions. This section will also include a Wrap Up portion, which concludes the group session and leads to the Reflect section.

REFLECT: This at-home study section helps you dig deeper into Scripture and apply the truths you're learning. Go deeper each week by reading the suggested chapters in the book *The New Dare to Discipline* and completing the activities at the end of each session in this study.

Guidelines for Groups

While you can complete this study alone, you will benefit greatly from covering the material with your spouse or with the interaction of a Sunday school class or small group. Here are a few ways to cultivate a valuable experience as you engage in this study.

PREPARATION: To get the most out of each group time, read through the study each week and answer the questions so you're ready to discuss the material. It will also be helpful for you and your group members to have copies of the book *The New Dare to Discipline* (ISBN 978-1-4143-9135-9). Read it in advance of the study to prepare, and encourage your members to read the corresponding chapters each week. In your group, don't let one or two people shoulder the entire responsibility for conversation and participation. Everyone can pitch in and contribute.

CONFIDENTIALITY: In the study, you will be prompted to share thoughts, feelings, and personal experiences. Accept others where they are without judgment. Many of the challenges discussed will be private. These should be kept in strict confidence by the group.

RESPECT: Participants must respect each other's thoughts and opinions, providing a safe place for those insights to be shared without fear of judgment or unsolicited advice (including hints, sermons, instructions, and scriptural Band-Aids®). Take off your fix-it hat and leave it at the door, so you can just listen. If advice is requested, then it's okay to lend your opinion, seasoned with grace and offered with love.

ACCOUNTABILITY: Each week, participants will be challenged in their intentional parenting of their children. Commit to supporting and encouraging each other during the sessions and praying for each other between meetings.

Introduction

Have you ever stopped to consider all of the hats you wear as a parent?

There's your coach's hat for when you volunteer to take the literal role of soccer coach or batting instructor, but also the figurative one you wear when coaching your children to use things like the potty, kind words, or their bicycle hand brakes. There's the EMT hat you wear when you become the medical first responder for all sorts of literal bumps and bruises, but also the figurative ones when your child experiences hurt feelings or a broken heart. There's the chief executive officer hat you put on when managing the daily resources, finances, and scheduling it takes to run the conglomerate that is your child's life.

This metaphor could go on way too long, but you get the idea. As a mom or dad of a child of any age, you take on an ever-growing set of enormous tasks. Consider the length of time any of these occupations requires: coach, EMT, CEO.

Before you became a parent, perhaps you were well prepared and you knew that one of the more important hats you would wear at each stage of your child's development would be that of disciplinarian. More likely, however, you underestimated the amount of time involved wearing this particular hat. There is discipline to be incorporated into every decision you make, every incident you encounter, and every opportunity you are given as a parent. Unfortunately, discipline itself is a very misunderstood term.

Discipline is both a noun and a verb. As a noun, *discipline* is defined as "control that is gained by requiring that rules or orders be obeyed and punishing bad behavior."[1] As a verb, *discipline* is defined as "to punish (someone) as a way of making sure that rules or orders are obeyed."[2]

In some ways, we associate discipline, the noun, only with punishment. It's so much more. You utilize discipline the verb in order to achieve discipline the noun. You must discipline your child so that he or she will become disciplined. Both the noun and the verb are essential in parenting.

Today, true biblical discipline as is under attack. It's an endangered species in the world of raising children. Modern philosophies, although sometimes empty and useless, tell you that disciplining according to God's Word harms a child psychologically when the exact opposite is true. Rather, it's the lack of biblical discipline that damages children.

Biblical precepts are timeless. There's no truth expressed in Scripture that worked thousands of years ago that doesn't work now. The inspired concepts in Scripture have been handed down from generation to generation and are just as valid for the twenty-first century as they were for our ancestors.

You're participating in this study because you want to raise your kids well. To develop healthy children, you and I need to move from simply a desire to achieve the perfect balance between boundaries and blessings to intentionally exploring biblically-based practices founded in God's Word.

The goal of this study is to expose you to the plan God establishes for you to discipline and disciple your children to be exactly who He designed them to be. You'll also be equipped with tools to establish a plan for shaping the will of your child without breaking his or her spirit.

The Bible doesn't give us one simple formula for raising perfect kids. We are sinful, and so are our children. What the Bible does offer, though, is fundamental guidelines for us as parents. Because each child is different, each exercise in discipline will be different. Consider this: two carpenters can be given the exact same tools and build wildly different pieces of furniture, both as beautiful as they are useful, but different nonetheless. The tools exposed by this study are exactly that, tools to use. It's up to you, by the power of God, to create something beautiful and useful for Him. So let's get to work!

1. "Discipline," *Merriam-Webster* (online), [cited 23 May 2014]. Available from the Internet: *www. merriam-webster.com*.
2. Ibid.

WEEK 1

MIND
· · · · · · · · · · · ·
THE GATE

● **BEFORE YOU BEGIN,** take time to pray with your group. Ask God to teach the group how to be proactive, loving parents to their children just as He is to us.

Boundaries are everywhere. Countries have borders. Yards have fences. Boundaries keep people in and they also keep people out. Many might suppose that boundaries limit freedom. Consider, however, who is more free? The puppy who has a fenced yard in which to play with no threat of danger or the dog who was hit by a car because the gate was left open? Boundaries don't limit our freedom. Boundaries protect our freedom.

> Name rules, boundaries, or limits that were present in your home when you were growing up.

> Did you push back against those boundaries? Why or why not?

> Do you feel like those boundaries were arbitrary and/ or controlling, or for your own benefit?

The truth about children is that they thrive in situations where they know and understand limits. Children claim their sense of security from appropriate limits. The fact that they often push those limits isn't always an indication that they don't like boundaries or that rules are bad. There are times when a child, because of his inborn nature, will clench his little fists and dare his parents to accept his challenges. He isn't motivated by frustration or inner hostility, as it's often supposed. He merely wants to know where the boundaries lie and who's available to enforce them.

WATCH CLIP 1 from the study DVD and answer the following questions:

> Other than the anger that was mentioned, what do you use to motivate your children to obey?

> What does losing control look like for you?

Some parents determine that it's best not to enforce too many rules or set too many limits for their children. They may be under the assumption that those rules could be seen as an effort to control their children in a totalitarian way. In part, this could be due to their own desire to parent in a way that is different than how they were parented. Instead of being an effort to obtain authoritative control over children, discipline is your best attempt to implant self-control in them. These parents may be under the impression that limits will stifle the energy, creativity, and the unique personality of their child. Instead, boundaries provide the proper foundation for every unique part of a child to thrive and grow in healthy ways.

> Looking back now, how do you feel about the overall sense of boundaries (how they were determined, communicated, and enforced) in your home growing up?

> How do you set those same boundaries?
> Have you avoided setting boundaries? If so, why?

Let's examine what the Bible says about boundaries and limits concerning discipline in the home. Without a biblical rationale for discipline, all the tips and ideas probably won't work. Unless you know the "why" of discipline, the "how" won't matter. The "why" is what maintains strong motivation and resolve when the "how" proves difficult.

● **CONTINUE YOUR GROUP TIME** with this discussion guide.

The design of a family according to the very Word of God includes parents. A man and woman become one flesh (see Gen. 2:24) and together are fruitful. They multiply (see Gen. 1:28) by the birth of children. Then Scripture instructs this man and woman about their role as parents.

● **READ** Deuteronomy 6:1-9.

> What do these verses explain as the responsibility of parents to children regarding faith?

Verse 4 is known as the Shema. It's the declaration of faith for God's people Israel and the recognition of the oneness of God. This dimension of God's character is given further credibility when the first of the Commandments is an admonition to put no other gods before Him. Deuteronomy 6:5 explains how people are to respond to this God—with love. When parents respond to God in love, they teach their children to reproduce that love of God in the next generation. Multiplying is more than producing children. It's also producing faith in children.

> What do verses 1-3 tell us about God's expectation for His people?

God's people were to keep His statutes and commands (verse 2) and follow them (verse 3). In verse 6, when God says, "these words," the reader can assume that God means all of the commands and statutes that He communicated in His law and above that, the expectation that people heed those words in an attitude of worship toward Him.

In verses 1-3, God tells His people to keep His commands. In verse 5, God tells His people they are to love Him completely. Jesus blends the two together in John 14:15 saying, "If you love Me, you will keep My commands." Love and obedience are the closest of friends. And God's design for parents is a loving, obedient relationship with their children.

What does it look like to love God and to obey His Word completely?

● **READ** Ephesians 6:4.

What does this verse say about the purpose of parental discipline?

Limits and boundaries are an effort to train and teach. Godly discipline is a necessary part of teaching children to obey the Lord. God expects parents to obey His commands and to teach children to do the same.

● **READ** Ephesians 6:1-3.

What is God's expectation for children?

Ephesians 6:3 clarifies the difference between the 5th Commandment in the Decalogue (the only one of the Ten Commandments that comes with a promise) and the preceding commands.

According to verse 3, what is the reason for children to be obedient to their parents?

How does that reason fit with what God told His people in Deuteronomy 6:3?

God's motivation behind His desire for obedience is for our benefit. How generous is He, at the establishment of His relationship with the Hebrew nation, to tell them what is best for them!

You've certainly heard the phrase, "I want what is best for my kids." As a good parent, you've likely said that phrase a time or two. The issue with that phrase isn't the intent behind it, but instead the meaning of just one word within it. *Best*.

What is best and who decides that?

Check what the world says is best for your kids?
☐ Education   ☐ Popularity
☐ Well-rounded life ☐ Friends
☐ Opportunities   ☐ Other: _____

Obedience to the Lord leads to what is best for you. And the best for your children is to live in submission to you, as you submit to the Lord.

● **READ** Hebrews 12:5-11.

How are love and discipline tied together in this verse?

Discipline is what's best for your children. Discipline underscores your love for them. Disciplinary action isn't an assault on parental love; it's the proof of it. Appropriate punishment isn't something parents do *to* a beloved child; it's something that's done *for* them.

You demonstrate your love for God when you obey Him. You show love for your children when you call them to obey you. You even prove your love for them when you punish them in response to their disobedience.

Again, boundaries don't limit your freedom. They protect it. Setting proper boundaries is among the best things you can do for them. And yes, this is difficult at times—for you and for your child. (See Heb. 12:11.) We all would likely prefer an easier way, but it wouldn't be the best way. The reason behind setting limits and disciplining your children is that you love them and it's what is best for them. With this as your proper motivation, you can stick to the hard task of godly discipline, because you know that in the end, it leads to more joy in parenting.

THIS WEEK'S INSIGHTS

• • •

- Boundaries are for your good and the good of your children.
- Consistent, godly discipline is what is best for your children.
- Discipline is an indication of God's love for you just as obedience is an indication of your love for Him.

Considering the age of your children, how can you best communicate your reason for disciplining them this week?

How can you best help them know why discipline is an important part of your love for God and for them?

WRAP UP

• • •

PRAY TOGETHER asking God to reveal ways to set boundaries for your children in order to show them love. Ask Him to shape your heart to discipline them in this Godlike way.

Dear Father, who disciplines His children out of love, thank You. Thank You for the moments of discipline and pruning in our lives. Help us obey You as a demonstration of our love for You. Help us call our children to obedience as an expression of our love for them. We cannot raise them apart from Your divine leading so we trust in You. Amen.

- **READ AND COMPLETE** the activities for this section before your next group time. For further insight, read chapters 1, 7, and 10 from the book *The New Dare to Discipline.*

THE FAITH BEHIND DISCIPLINE

First, the goal of parenting is passing faith on to your children.

- **READ** Deuteronomy 6:4-9.

> Consider all of the moments you have throughout the week to teach your children about God. Do you leverage every opportunity available? How so or why not?

> When do you spend the most time helping your children focus on God and learn biblical truth?

> Consider the following chart and the opportunities you have throughout the day to be a teacher, friend, coach, or counselor. What are other ways you might wear those hats to accomplish the accompanying goals?[1]

TIMES	COMMUNICATION	ROLE	GOAL
Meal Time	Formal Discussion	Teacher	Establish Values
Drive Time	Informal Dialogue	Friend	Interpret Life
Bed Time	Intimate Conversation	Counselor	Build Intimacy
Morning Time	Encouraging Words	Coach	Instill Purpose

When we spend time with our children—having fun and enjoying laughter and joy together—savoring moments of love and closeness, they will likely be tempted to test the limits. Many confrontations can be avoided by building a trusting relationship with kids and thereby helping them want to cooperate at home

> In the context of a week filled with school, work, church, and extracurricular activities, when do you have the most concentrated quality time with your kids?

Here are a couple of tips on how you can create more of this quality time with your children:

TIP 1. If you're too busy to create these quality experiences, evaluate your time commitments and consider what you could cut out in order to refocus your family energy on Christ and one another. If there's nothing you can give up, consider how you might leverage the time you spend doing other things to create more fun and more teachable moments along the way.

TIP 2. Don't get caught up worrying about the overall quantity of time. There's a misconception that an increase in the quantity of time you spend with your kids automatically improves the quality of that time. It's not enough to spend an increasing amount of time with them if that time is not strategic or meaningful.[2]

THE LOVING AUTHORITY BEHIND DISCIPLINE

● **READ** Hebrews 12:5-11 and Proverbs 3:11-12.

Effective parenting is one of the toughest jobs you'll ever have. Godly parenting is rarely promoted as being easy, but instead very challenging. Facing those challenges with courage and resolve is always worth it.

According to Hebrews 12:10, what's the difference between the discipline of an earthly father and God the Father?

According to verse 11, what's the desired outcome of godly discipline?

One of your discipline goals should be that your children will be obedient to God. You have to ask yourself if your motivation for having obedient children is wrapped up more in what is convenient for you or what is pleasing to God and therefore best for them.

Tedd Tripp gives this warning in his book *Shepherding a Child's Heart*:

> Parenting goals are often no more noble than immediate comfort and convenience. When parents require obedience because they feel under pressure, obedience of children is reduced to parental convenience.[3]

There are many moments when being a disciplinarian will be very difficult. Not only is it difficult because it's painful for the very kids you would die for, but it's also challenging because it requires time, thought, energy, and commitment. You don't wake up in the morning, glance at your schedule for the day, and notice specifically calendared moments to discipline your children. You likely don't plan for moments of disobedience. They usually pop up unexpectedly. This means you need to be ready when they occur.

Generally speaking, your children came with an inborn propensity for disobedience. By their very sinful nature, they'll disobey when you have time to respond immediately and when you're busy and would rather not bother. Even when it's inconvenient, you must be prepared to invoke appropriate consequences and teach important lessons when your children give you reason.

● **READ** Genesis 18:19.

> Why did God specifically choose Abraham and what was Abraham set apart to do regarding his children?

> Generally speaking, do you find the culture of the parents in your sphere of community to be more disciplinarian or more permissive in nature?
> How does that impact your parenting?

Children thrive best in an atmosphere of love, undergirded by reasonable, consistent discipline. You're in charge. There must be no confusion about the authority in your child's life. You don't exercise this control to yield power, achieve status, or manipulate them. You're an extension of God in their life directing them toward what is right, holy, and pleasing to Him. If you're committed to your own obedience to God's call, you gladly accept this authority. This comes from the overwhelming love you feel for your child, and out of your strong desire to do what's best for them.

Failing to discipline your children is abdicating the role and responsibility God has given you as a parent. It's as if you are willfully rejecting His specific plan for your life in favor of your own comfort and ease.

PARENT CHALLENGE

INTERVIEW YOUR KIDS. Ask them about discipline. Use the following questions as a guide.

- How do you feel when we correct you when you're disobedient?
- Do you understand why we punish you for breaking rules?
- Do you understand our guidelines and what we expect from you, or are you sometimes surprised by the things we correct?
- Do you understand how our correction means we love you, or do you feel like we're angry and love you less when you're disciplined?

ARTICULATE YOUR THOUGHTS. Complete the following sentences and consider how you might use them to better explain expectations and discipline to your children. All of your reasons should give preference to God and His Word about what is best for your children.

- I choose to discipline you because ...
- I choose to discipline you because ...
- I choose to discipline you because ...

MAKE IT A MEMORY. Post these verses in a prominent place. Use them as reminders of your call, your place, and your purpose as a parent.

- Genesis 18:19
- Ephesians 6:4
- Hebrews 12:11
- Proverbs 3:11-12

PERSONAL REFLECTION
• • •

You set boundaries for a reason. The discipline you use when boundaries are inevitably crossed, is vital to raising godly children. Commit yourself to consistent, biblically-centered discipline for the purpose of training them to follow God and passing faith to the next generation.

> Compose a list in the space below of all the goals you might seek to accomplish in disciplining your children.

....

....

> Read Hebrews 12:10 and Proverbs 3:11-12 one more time. What do each of these passages confirm about the genuine goal of godly discipline?

....

....

---

1. Reggie Joiner, *Think Orange* (Colorado Springs: David C Cook, 2009), 69.
2. Ibid.
3. Tedd Tripp, *Shepherding a Child's Heart* (Wapwallopen, PA: Shepherd Press, 1995), 29.

WEEK 2

THE SUN
ALWAYS
· · · · · · · · · · · · · · · · ·
SETS

● **START YOUR GROUP TIME** by discussing what participants discovered in their Reflect homework.

When was the last time you were in an argument with someone, and you were most definitely right? Perhaps it was a disagreement with your child, perhaps your spouse. Maybe you were arguing with a neighbor, coworker, or friend. Regardless of the scuffle, only consider the last one where you were right.

How did you handle yourself in that situation?

Did you lose your temper and say words you didn't mean?

Did you end up apologizing in the end?

In any situation, losing your temper forfeits your right to be right. Do you understand that concept? Anger is not a sin, but letting your anger control your actions is. When your anger gets the best of you, it wins, and your being right no longer matters.

In the countless cases of disciplinary charges you bring against your children, you are probably right more often than not.

- Zach should not hit his sister.
- Candace may not use your cosmetics without asking.
- Sam must finish his homework before playing video games.
- Ella may not speak to you in that tone of voice.

You could add to that small list of examples. Disciplining a child in any of those circumstances and the myriad of others that easily come to mind is essential. You are right in those moments to correct behavior and enact appropriate consequences. The trouble comes when you lose your temper and when anger controls your thoughts, words, and actions.

● **WATCH CLIP 2** from the study DVD and answer the following questions:

> Discuss why your child responding obediently to anger doesn't accomplish a good result.

> What alternatives, in addition to the one mentioned in the clip, can help you avoid becoming angry?

> Why is it important for you to be in control of both your child and your own emotions at the same time?

When you give in to sin because of your anger and frustration, you forfeit your right to be right. Instead of being the mom who enforced the rules, you're the mom who yelled. Instead of being the dad who punished a misbehaving child, you're the dad who exasperated your son and created an unhealthy fear in him.

> List common expressions of anger a parent might resort to when dealing with children.

> Place a check mark by those that you have succumbed to in your time as a parent.

Anger may be a natural emotion or feeling when your children fail to obey. It may be your first feeling when they make choices that don't reflect Christ or the manner in which you have instructed them to live. Anger is certainly natural, but acting in anger undercuts discipline. Disciplining out of anger does nothing to accomplish the desired objective. In this session, you'll discover some important truths about anger and learn the importance of keeping your anger under control when it comes to discipline.

● **CONTINUE YOUR GROUP TIME** with this discussion guide.

Having parenting goals is important. Striving toward having obedient, careful, and respectful children is worthwhile. A key point, however, is not to focus too much on making your children compliant. It must be for them to become Christlike. Likewise, your goal must not be to turn them into adults before they're adults. They can be Christlike kids who obey you and not lose their childlikeness. Conversely, another destructive attitude in parenting is overlooking any and all bad behaviors with the excuse, "Well, kids will be kids."

> In what ways does today's culture pressure your children to be perfect (grades, sports, media)?

> In what ways do you demand perfection from your kids? Do you find yourself demonstrating anger if results aren't immediately seen?

As we discuss how to respond to your children when discipline is needed, reflect back on how we responded to common expressions of anger. Do you see this kind of speech come out in times of correcting your children? Let's see what the Bible has to say about that kind of speech.

● **READ** Proverbs 15:1.

> How might this verse be dangerously misinterpreted to lead a parent to the absence of discipline?

> What wisdom does this verse offer about how you speak when disciplining your child?

It's important to know the difference between raising your voice and yelling. Volume speaks value. You wouldn't quietly request that your child move away from the road when they're inches from traffic. Screaming, "No! Step back!" would be completely appropriate. A raised voice sometimes communicates urgency and importance. However, yelling at your child for something they've done wrong is entirely different.

Dr. Jim Burns gives the following wisdom on yelling:

> "Yelling crushes and shuts down your child's spirit. The more you yell, the less they hear. The message your children will hear if you are yelling is that you are mad at them; they won't hear the meaning of your words. ... Parents who resort to yelling will find it not only upsetting, but also ineffective."[1]

There's a difference between bad behavior and childlike behavior. Both require discipline. Neither warrants exasperation. The trouble with anger is that it doesn't motivate. It doesn't achieve the desired result, but instead produces what no good parents would ever want—a hurt child.

How have you been hurt by someone's anger? Were you motivated to change or driven to anger yourself?

Is anger a sin? Why or why not?

● **READ** Ephesians 4:26.

The Bible assumes that we will become angry. It doesn't even tell us that anger is a sin. It does, however, instruct us to not sin in our anger. Anger itself isn't sinful. The outbursts and accusations that usually accompany anger are sinful and according to Ephesians 4, should be avoided. Anger is a natural emotion, and also a very powerful one, that must be controlled.

● **READ** James 1:19-20.

What are the things your kids do, or don't do, that brings about anger?

How many of those things, if left unchecked, will lead your child to ruin? How many are simply annoying?

If your motivation behind discipline is to correct behavior for the purpose of instilling values, illustrating God's love and justice, and moving your child from disobedience to obedience, anger won't accomplish that purpose. The goal isn't fearful compliance but a genuine shaping of your child's will.

● **READ** Numbers 14:18.

Combine the character of God expressed in Numbers 4:18 with the instruction James gives us in James 1:19. Just because God is patient and slow to anger, rich in love and forgiveness, doesn't mean that He doesn't punish sin. To overlook iniquity would make God a hypocrite. He reigns in complete justice and in complete love. As parents, we are to be the same: slow to anger and quick to show love and forgiveness.

● **READ** Colossians 3:8, 12-14.

How do you combat your issues with anger?

Ultimately, anger only serves to reveal your own sin. It doesn't correct the behavior in your child. When your own temper complicates disciplining your children, they can't possibly learn the lesson you desire to teach. Anger is Satan's best chance at inciting an outburst out of you and marring the way you represent God's love and justice to your child. He is doubly effective when he causes you to stumble and prevents your child from learning, all because of an out-of-control temper.

In reality, disobedience to his parent reveals a problem between the child and God. That is the bigger issue. More than making you angry, it should raise concern about the bigger issue of your child's heart and how it's being shaped. Discipline then isn't an exercise in correcting behavior, but shaping your child to know and follow God.

THIS WEEK'S INSIGHTS
• • •

- Angry outbursts forfeit your right to be right and compromise your attempt at disciplining your child.
- Anger itself is not a sin, but a natural emotion that must be tempered so that it does not take control.
- The best wisdom from Scripture regarding anger is for you to be slow to allow it, then diligent to remove it from your life, replacing it with godly character and love.

Everyone deals with anger to some degree or another. Would you say you control your anger or does your anger typically control you?

What outbursts do you need to repent from and seek forgiveness for from your children?

WRAP UP
• • •

PRAY TOGETHER making informed decisions about who God wants you to be, and commit yourself more fully to walking with Him.

Dear Father, we're sinful people, completely deserving of Your anger, yet receiving Your love and forgiveness. Even in Your discipline, You offer us Your mercy. Teach us to do the same for our children. Amen.

● **READ AND COMPLETE** the activities for this section before your next group time. For further insight, read chapters 2 and 3 from the book *The New Dare to Discipline.*

This week's group session likely unearthed some significant feelings in you regarding anger. Everyone has an experience with the emotion. You're either more linked to your own anger or more closely linked to someone else's anger directed toward you. In either case, it's a misunderstood emotion that often leaves a dramatic wake of damage.

THE LORD'S ANGER

Remember that anger isn't sin. There are good reasons to be angry. Some things should make you very angry, so much so that if you don't find your blood boiling, something else may be wrong. The Lord Himself exhibited strong moments of anger in Scripture.

● **READ** the following references and note what it is that made the Lord angry in each passage.

Numbers 32:10-13

Deuteronomy 32:16-19

1 Kings 11:9-10

2 Chronicles 36:16

There are countless other examples. To put it in simple terms, God hates sin. What kind of God would He be if He didn't? God is diametrically opposed to evil.

● **READ** Psalm 7:11.

What does this verse reveal about the nature of God's anger?

Very plainly, God is righteous and therefore His anger and any display of it He chooses is completely justified. His very nature won't allow for the possibility of excusing sin and iniquity. So rather than accept it or excuse it, in His divine love, He atoned for it through the death of His own Son. Fortunately for us, God's anger is slow (see Ps. 103:8), often turned away (see Ps. 78:38), and ultimately satisfied by the death of Jesus. (See 1 John 4:10)

In the Old Testament, there were many moments where God's wrath was poured out on His own people and also the enemies of God's people in order to fulfill God's purpose (See Ex. 33:18–34:7; Deut. 28:15-68; Num. 16.) His wrath was poured out on all sin. You're not left with the question about God's wrath for today. But while His righteous anger still burns against sin, and while consequences still abound in response to sin, God's wrath was satisfied by the cross.

Reflect on the sin you've been forgiven of. Take a moment to understand the weight of God's anger against you because of your sin, and the blessing of God's mercy toward you through Jesus.

YOUR ANGER

● **READ** Psalm 30:5 and Matthew 5:21-24.

What does Psalm 30:5 say very specifically about divine anger and divine favor?

What is it that really makes you angry?

What do the verses in Matthew teach you about anger?

Allowing anger to control your actions impedes your worship. Jesus instructs the man to make things right with the person he wronged before coming back to make his sacrifice to God.

Consider for a moment the relationship you have with your kids. Has an angry outburst, cleverly disguised as your preferred method of discipline, exasperated your children and turned them against you? Rather than loving and respecting you, are they now operating out of an unhealthy fear of your anger against them?

If this is so, the Bible is clear. Your worship is weakened. Jesus says to stop what you're doing to honor Him and first be made right to the one you wronged—including your kids. Not only do you honor God when you admit you're wrong and restore the broken fellowship you have with Him, you also model that behavior for your kids. They'll learn to repent of their own faults by watching you in moments when you confess yours.

WHAT GOES IN MUST COME OUT

● **READ** Luke 6:43-45 and Philippians 4:6-9.

> What does the passage in Luke indicate about the place where evil actions and words come from in your life?

> How is worry present in your life as a parent?

Worry leads to anger while unchecked anger can mask a deep sense of worry. Did you know that? Do you see how one can so easily contribute to the other? When there's peace and trust in your heart, you are full and there's no room for anger or frustration. Consider the mom who is worried about her children's behavior around other moms. There's an appearance that she's constantly worried about not fulfilling. What happens when her kids don't cooperate and help her maintain that appearance? She becomes frustrated and angry. She acts in haste, out of fear and selfishness, with no regard to what she is teaching her children in the process. Worry has now erupted in anger.

Now consider the dad on the sidelines who constantly yells at his superstar athlete. The father's expectation is that the child will constantly improve, never have an off moment, and never ever lose. What is the worry? Fear that his child won't measure up. Fear that the child won't succeed. Fear that it's an indication of his own failure. Fear that the child will end up in a situation like his. And all of his fears are hidden by his angry demeanor.

Worry and anger are certainly not twins, but they are definitely cousins from the same family line.

> **What kinds of things do you worry about?**

> **Does your need to manage those things ever manifest itself in severe frustration or mask itself in anger? Explain.**

> **Look back at Philippians 4. What does Paul instruct his people to focus on instead of their worry or doubt?**

Consider your own outbursts of anger for a moment. Have you ever asked yourself why you get that way, especially when so many of the things that make you angry might be so trivial? Why sticky toothpaste residue in the sink sends you over the edge? Why getting out of bed three times before falling asleep is the object of your rage? When it comes to parenting your children, parenting out of anger or frustration is never God-honoring.

PERSONAL REFLECTION
• • •

Asking why you react the way you do to the anger you're experiencing is not only appropriate for children but for parents too. Doing this will help get to the heart of the matter. And ultimately, if the goal of discipline is shaping the child's heart without breaking the child's spirit, a parent needs to understand their own heart and the heart of their child.

Consider the list of things that make you angry. What is your default behavior when it comes to being angry? Answer the following questions about the actions that typically result from your anger.

What were you feeling when you ...?

What was done to make you respond in anger?

How did your acting out in anger make it better?

In what other way could you have responded?

Consider using these same questions with your children when they act inappropriately in anger. These four simple questions help you understand yourself and your child better. Then together, you can ask God to remove fear, worry, doubt, and anger from your hearts, and to fill you with good things like love, encouragement, patience, and joy.

---

1. Jim Burns, *Confident Parenting* (Bloomington: Bethany House Publishers, 2007), 132.

PICK YOUR BATTLE WITH THE **END** IN MIND

● **START YOUR GROUP TIME** by discussing what participants discovered in their Reflect homework.

Some say that their greatest goal is to make their children happy. So the best strategy to make your children happy is to create environments that cultivate happiness. If candy makes them happy in the moment, give them candy. If doing their homework assignments for them makes them happy, get out your No. 2 pencil.

As parents, you must surrender the idea that your purpose is to make your children happy. Yes, there will be moments where happiness is the product of your good parenting, but it's definitely not the end goal.

> **In your opinion, what is the purpose of disciplining your children?**

One also might conclude that having compliant children who listen and obey well is the goal. Actually, that is a happy by-product of the goal. The purpose of disciplining your children isn't to make them compliant; it's to move them toward Christlikeness. And since you can't change your child's heart, the best way to create Christlike behavior in your kids is to model Christlike behavior for your kids.

God has given us the assignment of representing Him during the formative years of parenting. That's why it's so critically important for us to acquaint our kids with God's two predominant natures— His unfathomable love and His justice.

> **What does God's unfathomable love look like?**

> **What does God's justice look like?**

> **How do you illustrate both to your kids by your actions?**

● **WATCH CLIP 3** from the study DVD and answer the following questions:

Have you ever used a similar system of checkpoints mentioned in the video? If so, have you seen a benefit to using it?

If not, what kinds of disciplinary systems do you use instead?

Where do you fall on the following two continuums of consequence? Give explanations with your answers.

DISCIPLINARY CONSEQUENCES

Made up on the spot   Pre-determined

DISCIPLINARY ACTION

Follows through   offers additional chances

What surprises you the most from the answers given?

● **CONTINUE YOUR GROUP TIME** with this discussion guide.

What makes you happy?

Do these things that make you happy also draw you closer to Christ? Why or why not?

Some things you listed are likely very kin to your relationship with Christ. These draw you deeper into a personal walk with Him and strengthen your resolve to follow Him more intentionally. These do more than make you happy. They make you joyful. Other things on your list, however, are just temporary fixes. They make you happy for a moment but when the relationship, circumstance, or feelings end or change, the happiness wanes.

Now what if you were asked about pain or suffering—if these things made you happy? It would be an odd response if you answered yes. But although pain and suffering don't provide pleasure, they can accomplish something in us that does bring ultimate joy.

● **READ** Hebrews 12:6-7, 11.

What do these verses say about punishment regarding pain?

Can you think of a moment in your life when you experienced pain and suffering, but looking back you know it was the Lord's discipline in your life?

● **READ** Philippians 3:8-10.

According to Paul, how should we view this kind— or any kind—of suffering?

An incorrect view of God might be that He desires to end all suffering and protect us and our children from all pain. Instead, He invites us to share in the suffering of Jesus. Another incorrect view of God might be that He sits in heaven on a cosmic throne distributing pain, seeking out sinners to punish, and taking pleasure in their demise. Verse 6 says that the Lord disciplines those He loves. Verse 7 follows by explaining that when God disciplines people, He is treating them as His children.

How have you experienced discipline from the Lord?

How have you seen positive steps in your child's life as a result of discipline from the Lord or from you?

Pain is a good thing. Pain receptors in our body send messages to our brain, which triggers important reactions. If you touch something hot, the pain causes you to jerk your hand back. If you didn't feel pain, you might be content to leave your hand on a hot stove. Pain is a helpful message. The memory of pain reminds us not to repeat the same mistakes. The same happens when we experience emotional pain.

How can a healthy approach to dealing with emotional pain and suffering be good for your children?

How can protecting children from appropriate levels of pain be damaging to them long-term?

Sometimes being too cautious does more harm than good. Protecting children from pain can actually have an adverse affect. If children never experience pain because of overprotective parents, they won't learn how to make wise choices and ultimately protect themselves. Protecting children from the consequences of their actions fosters in them an attitude where their actions don't matter. Pain and suffering are important teachers. Consequences are important lessons.

● **READ** Galatians 6:7-10.

> Discuss the concept of sowing and reaping as a group. How do you see this truth played out in everyday life?

There is certainly a law of cause and effect present in this world that God created. But it's certainly not absolute, at least not in this life.

● **READ** Romans 9:14-15.

> In what ways have you experienced God's mercy or the withholding of consequences that you deserved or His gracious reward that you did not?

> Why is it important that your children experience both the law of sowing and reaping and the blessing of God's undeserved mercy and grace?

Once again, the secret is balance. It's not healthy to be overprotective—or completely permissive. God's parenting style exemplifies this principle perfectly. Sometimes He allows us to fall and struggle and learn on our own, but He's always there to pick us up and show us mercy and compassion. You'll have to discover when to rescue your child and when to stand at a distance.

Parenting well involves making choices. Some things are worth fighting for. When you choose your battles, choose the ones that will help you your children move toward holiness, not necessarily happiness. Is drawing a line in the sand best for your child or will a dose of mercy be more effective? As a parent, you are called to demonstrate God's character to your children by showing His love and His justice.

THIS WEEK'S INSIGHTS

• • •

- Children must be shown the love and the justice of God.
- Consistent and appropriately applied discipline shows your children a side of God's character that they wouldn't otherwise see, and it gives them a better understanding of the concept of sowing and reaping.
- Sparing your children every level of pain and suffering is ultimately shielding them from fully knowing and trusting God.

Describe the ways the world views pain and suffering.

Consider the following quote from C. S. Lewis:

> We can ignore even pleasure. But pain insists upon being attended to. God whispers to us in our pleasures, speaks in our conscience, but shouts in our pains: it is his megaphone to rouse a deaf world.[1]

How do you use suffering as teachable moments?

WRAP UP

• • •

PRAY TOGETHER asking God to help you find the balance in mercy and justice with your discipline.

> Lord, Your Word is a light unto our path to guide our way. It helps us understand pain and difficulty in this life from Your perspective rather than the world's. Help us to choose wisely regarding the discipline of our children. Help us to leverage circumstances, happy ones and hard ones, to show them You. Help us discipline so they may know You and follow You. Amen.

● **READ AND COMPLETE** the activities for this section before your next group time. For further insight, read chapters 5 and 6 from the book *The New Dare to Discipline.*

As you start this Reflect section, refer to the definitions of discipline, the verb, and discipline, the noun, on page 7 of the introduction. Without one, you can't fully achieve or appreciate the other. You must have discipline the verb in order to achieve discipline the noun.

THE DISCIPLINE OF DISCIPLESHIP

Proverbs 19:18 reads, "Discipline your son while there is hope; don't be intent on killing him." In the Gospels, Jesus asked what good parent would give their child a snake when he asked for fish. (See Matt. 7:10.) While the world continues to promote that clear boundaries and heavy discipline squelch a child, God's Word reminds us yet again that to withhold proper discipline is to ruin your child.

> Look again at the definitions of discipline. Compose your own definition of both in the spaces below:
>
> Discipline, the verb:
>
>
> Discipline, the noun:

There's a word the church often uses to describe following Jesus. It's a word that sounds very much like the word *discipline*. Can you guess it? It's *discipleship*.

The word *disciple* is the Greek word *mathetes* and it literally means *learner*. It was a common distinction in the Jewish and Roman worlds of the New Testament. While Jesus wasn't the only leader with followers, the relationship that Jesus had with His disciples is the one we seek to understand and imitate.

What does the word *disciple* mean to you?

Paul said in 1 Corinthians 11:1, "Imitate me, as I also imitate Christ." Who makes you more like Christ?

If the goal of the believer is to be like Christ, what areas do you know you must improve upon embodying parts of Christ's character?

● **READ** and make time to memorize Philippians 2:1-5.

Not only is this passage to be the aim of your life, but also your aim as a parent for your child's life. There may or may not be things in this passage that need to be addressed in your own home. Does rivalry need to be harnessed? Does conceit need to be tempered? Does humility need to be expanded? Does selfless service need to be elevated?

Write three steps you'd like to take as a believer and as a parent to further Christlikeness in your home.

1.

2.

3.

DEVELOPING A PROPER PLAN

As a parent attempting to execute a biblical model for discipline, you have a myriad of good goals in mind. Your desire is to help your children learn to be self-disciplined in their choices. This means you must use discipline the verb if your child steps outside the limits you set for them. This also means you must equip them with the tools necessary to live out discipline the noun as they learn responsibility and self-control.

Read the following three verses and respond to the questions that accompany each.

Plans fail when there is no counsel,
but with many advisers they succeed.
PROVERBS 15:22

Who do you look to for wisdom and advice as a godly parent who has raised godly kids? Explain why you chose this person.

But a noble person plans noble things;
he stands up for noble causes.
ISAIAH 32:8

Compose two lists below. First: all the selfish, ungodly goals a parent might have for disciplining their children. Second: all of the noble goals for being a parent who uses a biblical model of discipline.
List 1:   List 2:

Use the space below to identify plans to help you achieve the goals from the second list.

TIPS ON PLANS

1. **DON'T REACT IN THE HEAT OF THE MOMENT.** You don't do your best planning in the heat of the moment. It's best to plan when you are removed from a disciplinary dilemma so that your decisions can be guided by proper perspective.

2. **YOUR BEST PLANS MUST INCLUDE YOUR SPOUSE.** If the two of you do not agree on the proper boundaries, strategies, and consequences for disobedience, your child has already won. If you're not on the same page, you have already forfeited the battle. Even in a co-parenting situation where you and the child's other parent are no longer married or involved, unity is essential. If your child is also being parented by a step-parent, you dramatically undercut their ability to help if you're all not on board with the same plan.

3. **ROOT ALL OF YOUR PLANS IN SCRIPTURE.** This consistency is important. Worldly wisdom is only valuable if it's in keeping with what the Bible says about raising children. Compare parenting ideas you hear about, no matter how great they seem, through a proper litmus test of Scripture. Your plans must reflect God's will and your deepest desire to honor Him in keeping with His Word and will.

4. **MAKE ALLOWANCES FOR PAIN AND FAILURE.** Your proper plan for parenting must include not only discipline which feels painful for a moment, but a certain allowance for pain and failure in your child's life. You are not doing your child any favors by protecting him or her from every disappointment or difficulty.

● **READ** 2 Corinthians 12:9-10.

Some parents need to be reminded that their children aren't perfect. As much as you relish telling your child how special he is or how she is uniquely one of a kind, your child also needs to know that they are sinners in need of a Savior. There's a very selfish generation of young adults entering the world feeling very entitled because they have lived a very safe, happy, problem-free life under the supervision of parents who have moved mountains to revolve the world around their children. Please hear this: Your children are special. They are uniquely made and wonderfully gifted. But they are also in desperate need of Jesus. Without a proper understanding of their overwhelming need for a Savior, they won't develop faith and a desire to walk with Christ. If struggle is part of the process of a child growing in faith and being made strong, parents must allow and even author appropriate disappointments and circumstances in the lives of their children.

Discipline will cause struggle and pain. But it's worth it. As a parent, you're the filter that determines the level of pain and suffering your child experiences in circumstance and also the discipline they receive in response to their sin. You may choose to shield them from any and all difficulty in this life or you may leverage pain for a greater purpose, to help them know God. In both instances, there is a greater good worth choosing. It's not the easy road, but it's the one worth treading. When you go this route, happiness isn't your goal. A Christlike child is your aim.

PERSONAL REFLECTION
• • •

Spend some time this week reflecting on the following questions.

Are there things you haven't said no to in the past but you need to start saying no to now? What are those things?

Think of barriers that can have the potential to thwart or impede your plans of consistent discipline and setting a Christlike example. List those barriers below.

1. C. S. Lewis, *The Problem of Pain* (New York: HarperCollins, 1940), 91.

WEEK 4
WALKING
WORTHY
· ·

● **START YOUR GROUP TIME** by discussing what participants discovered in their Reflect homework.

You know the expressions. "Chip off the old block." "Following in his dad's footsteps." You undoubtedly possess a few characteristics that are reminiscent of your parents. Some are physical. Perhaps you have your mom's hair color or your dad's nose. Others are behavioral. Maybe you picked up your dad's punctuality or your mom's sense of humor. As you begin this final week, consider the good things that your parents passed on to you.

Jot down a few positive qualities or characteristics of your parents that are also true about you.

Are there interests, abilities, characteristics or attributes of yours that your children also share? Name a few.

Do your answers to these questions concern you? Do they delight you? Explain.

Apples don't fall far from trees. You're a product of the people and the place where you come from whether you like it or not. Your children will *most certainly* do the same. They'll often model your behavior, becoming who you are rather than whom you instruct them to be.

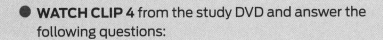

● **WATCH CLIP 4** from the study DVD and answer the following questions:

How did you feel listening to the letter from the adoptive mother?

Could you relate to her pain on any level or were you primarily relieved that your problems seem smaller in light of hers?

Remind yourself in the space below why love is such an important part of discipline and why discipline is such a vital part of love.

What does it mean to you to shape a child's will without crushing the child's spirit?

● **CONTINUE YOUR GROUP TIME** with this discussion guide.

Without delving into embarrassing American statistics about absentee fathers, suffice it to say that many children do not have proper role models in their homes. Maybe you grew up without a healthy image of marriage or helpful models of biblical manhood and womanhood. You certainly have an excuse for any attitudes and behaviors that have developed as a result, but be careful not to assume that excuse removes responsibility. The transforming love of Jesus and the instructions found in God's Word are more than enough to make up the difference for what you lacked in your home.

MEN: The way in which your sons grow up to treat women will be based on the way they watch you treat their mother. Your actions provide an example—good or bad.

WOMEN: The way in which your daughters learn to respect themselves and their future husbands will be based on the way they watch you treat their father. Your actions provide an example—good or bad.

SINGLE PARENTS: Be very aware of the way you are modeling respect with your co-parent. This is not without difficulty. However, without respect for one another even in situations of divorce, you fail to provide a proper model of respect for your children and thereby fail to deserve proper respect from your children.

How do these thoughts make you feel?

In what ways are you modeling respect and sacrifice as a single parent or in a marriage relationship?

When children learn to respect their parents, they'll also learn to respect others outside the home as well. A child's view of parental authority becomes the cornerstone of his or her outlook on school authority, law enforcement officers, employers, and countless others.

The parent-child relationship is the first and most important social interaction a youngster will have, and their training in obedience will often result in their being self-disciplined adults.

● **READ** Psalm 145:1-2.

> What do these two verses teach you in regard to respecting the Lord?

> Why is the concept of "every day" so important with regard to respect?

As a believer, you obey and respect the Lord and you show respect to others. As a Christ-following parent, God has given you positional authority over your kids and it is your duty to instruct them to obey. It is their responsibility to obey and respect you.

● **READ** Ephesians 4:1.

> Discuss what it means "to walk worthy of the calling you have received." What does walking worthy mean with regard to your calling as a parent?

If you want your children to respect others, you must demonstrate it rather than demand it. If you want your children to respect you, you must be worthy of it. Living your life in a manner deserving of respect not only gives reason for your children to offer it you, but also instills in them the very nature that will make them worthy of respect in return.

● **READ** Proverbs 20:7.

> Define *integrity*.

How are *respect* and *consistency* linked in your life as a believer?

● **READ** Proverbs 22:6.

Rewrite that proverb in your own words in the space provided and share it with your group.

There are many options for the way a child could go, but only one being the way they should go: the way of knowing and honoring the Lord. As a Christian parent, your desire should be to expose your children to the love of Jesus and to build faith and love for Christ in them. They're watching your own relationship with the Lord. Remember your children often associate their concept of a loving and just Heavenly Father with the way they view their earthly parents.

If Mom and Dad aren't worthy of respect, then neither are their morals, their values and beliefs, or even their faith. In many ways, the goal of parenting is letting go. One day, your child won't live under the umbrella of your constant care and supervision. We must model respect for God and others while our children are young, so they will do the same when they are living independently. If living a life of respect is valuable, it must be modeled, instructed, instilled, and appropriately reinforced through loving, consistent discipline.

THIS WEEK'S INSIGHTS
• • •

- You either provide your children with an example of how to live or an excuse for not living rightly before God with the way you demonstrate respect.
- Integrity in discipline is the best way to model godly behavior and respectful living.
- The manner in which respect is modeled to your children and caught by your children will be the manner in which they live respectfully as adults.

What concepts struck you as the most important throughout the entirety of this study?

Which ideas seem the most challenging?

Which ideas are you encouraged by most?

WRAP UP
• • •

PRAY TOGETHER that God would continue to allow you to discipline well.

> Heavenly Father, we care less about the small battles than the greater war. But we realize that the small battles do count toward overall victory. May we be parents who care more about Your glory than worldly standing, more about our children's faith than their momentary circumstances, and more about Your purpose for our lives than our own plans! Amen.

● **READ AND COMPLETE** the activities for this section before your next group time. For further insight, read chapters 8 and 9 from the book *The New Dare to Discipline.*

THE COST OF NOT DISCIPLINING YOUR CHILDREN

● **READ** 1 Samuel 2:12-17, 22-26.

The function of a priest in the community was to aid the people in worshiping the Lord. The sacrificial system set in motion by God in the Mosaic law clearly defined the role of those priests. When worshipers would bring a meat sacrifice, a portion was designated and given to the priests. (See Deut. 18:3.) Eli's sons were wicked men, not content with the prescribed amount, so they took more. According to the law, the fat was to be burned on the altar before the Lord (see Lev. 7:31), but Eli's sons demanded the fat for themselves in addition to the extra portion of raw meat. Their sin was exceedingly great before God.

● **READ** 1 Samuel 2:29.

By refusing to gain control of what his sons were doing, Eli essentially condoned their actions. Had he removed them from office and from the community for their sins, things might have ended differently. According to verse 29, God saw this act of permissive parenting as a direct violation of His Word. Eli chose his children over God. Big mistake!

In what ways do your children enhance your practice of faith and worship? Distract from it?

Do you feel like you condone outright sin against God from your children with an attitude of permissiveness?

View the following diagram and read the descriptions from Chip Ingram regarding multiple types of parenting:

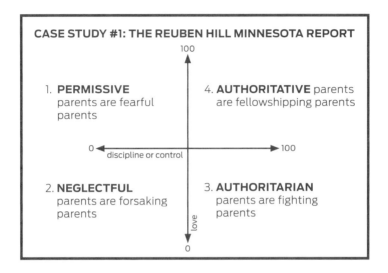

1. **THE PERMISSIVE PARENT.** The upper left quadrant represents parents who are high in love but low in discipline. The study revealed that permissive parents tend to produce children with very low self-esteem and feelings of inferiority. Though the parents express a lot of love, the lack of boundaries leaves their children with a high level of insecurity. Their parents are generally fearful, afraid of messing up and damaging their children's psyche, so they never set firm boundaries. The kids feel very loved yet very unsure of themselves.

2. **THE NEGLECTFUL PARENT.** The lower left quadrant belongs to the worst of all four combinations. This kind of parent doesn't express much love and also doesn't really care enough to discipline. Their children tend to grow up with little or no lasting relationship with Mom or Dad. The parents' neglect may not necessarily be intentional—they may simply be in the midst of their own traumas and chaos, like an addiction or an abusive situation. These children grow up with deep emotional scars, and their only hope is to find Christ and surround themselves with godly role models.

3. **THE AUTHORITARIAN PARENT.** The parent that shows up in the lower right quadrant doesn't express love and affection well but is very high on discipline. They raise children who are provoked to rebellion. The bar is always high and the "musts" are always abundant, so there's a strong sense of safety. But this kind of parent isn't content just to win the war; they have to win every battle too. Communication between parent and child takes the form of arguing and fighting. Authoritarian parents squeeze their kids until they can't wait to leave home, and as soon as they do, they rebel and potentially reject their faith altogether.

4. **THE AUTHORITATIVE PARENT.** Those who land in the upper right quadrant provide the best combination of love and discipline. This kind of parent is authoritative—not an overbearing authority, but a compassionate yet firm authority. They have clear boundaries and are also very loving. Everyone knows who the boss is, and there is a connection between parents and child, a consideration that respects and honors who the child is while not compromising his or her disciplinary needs. The result is a child high in self-esteem and equipped with good coping skills.[1]

Which quadrant do you most identify with regarding your parenting style?

Identify what motives or triggers drive you toward that quadrant.

If quadrant 4 isn't your primary style, identify what attitudes within you are keeping you from moving in that direction.

THE COST OF DISCIPLINING YOUR CHILDREN

Nothing in life apart from the saving grace of Jesus Christ is free. In fact, there's a cost attached immediately after one responds to Christ. When one becomes a disciple, there's a required sacrifice.

● **READ** Matthew 16:24.

The cross was a powerful symbol of death. It was a horrible form of public execution. Jesus invited anyone who would come with Him to die. Talk about sacrifice!

> What sacrifices have you made in order to follow Jesus?

> What are the costs associated with being in quadrant 4 as an authoritative parent?

When properly applied, loving discipline works! It stimulates tender affection, made possible by mutual respect between a parent and a child. It bridges the gap which otherwise separates family members who should love and trust each other. It allows the God of our ancestors to be introduced to our beloved children. It encourages a child to respect other people and live as a responsible, productive citizen. But as expected, there's a price tag on these benefits: they require courage, consistency, conviction, diligence, and enthusiastic effort. In short, one must dare to discipline in an environment of unmitigated love.

PARTING QUESTIONS

As you wrap up your time with this 4-week study, consider the following questions from each week's theme:

1. What does it look like to discipline your child out of love while desiring what is best for his or her life?

2. What next step will you take to continue learning about being your child's best parent and disciplining them in the most appropriate ways?

3. What issues must still be addressed in your life if you're to parent your child in a biblically sound manner with godly motives?

4. How can you pass this on to other parents? How can you offer them the same truths you have gleaned from this experience?

PERSONAL REFLECTION
• • •

Refer to the Key Insights from each session on the next page. In the space provided below, choose the one that resonates with you most from each session and record it below.

....

....

....

These are the truths that will stick with you as you go. Continually ask the Lord to set your heart on what it means to incorporate these truths into the daily decisions you make to raise godly sons and daughters into men and women who walk well with God.

1. Chip Ingram, "Effective Child Discipline," *Focus on the Family* (online), 2006 [cited 2 April 2014]. Available from the Internet: *www.focusonthefamily.com*.

Key Insights

WEEK 1

- Boundaries are for your good and the good of your children.
- Consistent, godly discipline is what is best for your children.
- Discipline is an indication of God's love for you just as obedience is an indication of your love for Him.

WEEK 2

- Angry outbursts forfeit your right to be right and compromise your attempt at disciplining your child.
- Anger itself is not a sin, but a natural emotion that must be tempered so that it does not take control.
- The best wisdom from Scripture regarding anger is for you to be slow to allow it, then diligent to remove it from your life, replacing it with godly character and love.

WEEK 3

- Children must be shown the love and the justice of God.
- Consistent and appropriately applied discipline shows your children a side of God's character that they wouldn't otherwise see, and it gives them a better understanding of the concept of sowing and reaping.
- Sparing your children every level of pain and suffering is ultimately shielding them from fully knowing and trusting God.

WEEK 4

- You either provide your children with an example of how to live or an excuse for not living rightly before God with the way you demonstrate respect.
- Integrity in discipline is the best way to model godly behavior and respectful living.
- The manner in which respect is modeled to your children and caught by your children will be the manner in which they live respectfully as adults.

Leader Notes

It's time for a leadership adventure. Don't worry; you don't have to have all the answers. Your role is to facilitate the group discussion, getting participants back on topic when they stray, encouraging everyone to share honestly and authentically, and guiding those who might dominate the conversation to make sure others are also getting some time to share.

As facilitator, take time to look over this entire study guide, noting the order and requirements of each session. Watch all the videos as well. Take time to read the suggested chapters (noted in the beginning of each Reflect section) from the book *The New Dare to Discipline* (ISBN 978-1-4143-9135-9). And pray over the material, the prospective participants, and your time together.

You have the option of extending your group's study by showing the films *Dare to Discipline* and *Your Legacy*. You can also keep it to four weeks by using just this study guide and DVD. The study is easy to customize for your group's needs.

Go over the How to Use This Study and the Guidelines for Groups sections with participants, making everyone aware of best practices and the steps of each session. Then dive into Week 1.

In establishing a schedule for each group meeting, consider ordering these elements for the hour of time together:

1. Connect—10 minutes
2. Watch—15 minutes
3. Engage—35 minutes

Be sure to allow time during each session to show the video clip. All four clips are approximately eight minutes or less in length. Reflect refers to the home study or activities done between group sessions.

Beginning with session 2, encourage some sharing regarding the previous week's Reflect home study. Usually at least one Connect question allows for this interaction. Sharing about the previous week's activities encourages participants to study on their own and be ready to share with their group during the next session.

As the study comes to a close, consider some ways to keep in touch. There may be some additional studies for which group members would like information. Some may be interested in knowing more about your church.

Occasionally, a group member may have needs that fall outside the realm of a supportive small group. If someone would be better served by the pastoral staff at your church or a professional counselor, please maintain a list of professionals to privately offer to that person, placing his/her road to recovery in the hands of a qualified pastor or counselor.

Use the space below to make notes or to identify specific page numbers and questions you would like to discuss with your small group each week based on their needs and season of life.

Further Resources

Need more guidance? Check out the following for help.

ON PARENTING:

The New Dare to Discipline by Dr. James Dobson
The New Strong-Willed Child by Dr. James Dobson
Bringing Up Boys by Dr. James Dobson
Bringing Up Girls by Dr. James Dobson
Dr. Dobson's Handbook of Family Advice by Dr. James Dobson
Raising Boys and Girls by Sissy Goff, David Thomas, and Melissa Trevathan
Love No Matter What by Brenda Garrison
Intentional Parenting by Sissy Goff, David Thomas, and Melissa Trevathan
Raising Girls by Melissa Trevathan and Sissy Goff
The Back Door to Your Teen's Heart by Melissa Trevathan
5 Love Languages by Gary Chapman
5 Conversations You Must Have with Your Daughter by Vicki Courtney
Parenting Teens magazine
HomeLife magazine
ParentLife magazine
The Parent Adventure by Selma and Rodney Wilson
Experiencing God at Home by Richard Blackaby and Tom Blackaby
Love Dare for Parents by Stephen Kendrick and Alex Kendrick
Authentic Parenting in a Postmodern Culture by Mary E. DeMuth
Grace-Based Parenting by Tim Kimmel

ON DISCUSSING FAITH WITH YOUR CHILDREN:

Your Legacy: The Greatest Gift by Dr. James Dobson
Bringing the Gospel Home by Randy Newman
Firsthand by Ryan Shook and Josh Shook
God Distorted by John Bishop
Sticky Faith by Dr. Kara E. Powell and Dr. Chap Clark
Parenting Beyond Your Capacity by Reggie Joiner and Carey Nieuwhof
A Praying Life by Paul Miller
Faith Conversations for Families by Jim Burns

Introducing Your Child to Christ

Your most significant calling and privilege as a parent is to introduce your children to Jesus Christ. A good way to begin this conversation is to tell them about your own faith journey.

Outlined below is a simple gospel presentation you can share with your child. Define any terms they don't understand and make it more conversational, letting the Spirit guide your words and allowing your child to ask questions and contribute along the way.

GOD RULES. The Bible tells us God created everything, and He's in charge of everything. (See Gen. 1:1; Col. 1:16-17; Rev. 4:11.)

WE SINNED. We all choose to disobey God. The Bible calls this sin. Sin separates us from God and deserves God's punishment of death. (See Rom. 3:23; 6:23.)

GOD PROVIDED. God sent Jesus, the perfect solution to our sin problem, to rescue us from the punishment we deserve. It's something we, as sinners, could never earn on our own. Jesus alone saves us. (See John 3:16; Eph. 2:8-9.)

JESUS GIVES. He lived a perfect life, died on the cross for our sins, and rose again. Because Jesus gave up His life for us, we can be welcomed into God's family for eternity. This is the best gift ever! (See Rom. 5:8; 2 Cor. 5:21; Eph. 2:8-9; 1 Pet. 3:18.)

WE RESPOND. Believe in your heart that Jesus alone saves you through what He's already done on the cross. Repent, by turning away from your sin. Tell God and others that your faith is in Jesus. (See John 14:6; Rom. 10:9-10,13.)

If your child is ready to respond, explain what it means for Jesus to be Lord of his or her life. Guide your child to a time in prayer to repent and express his or her belief in Jesus. If your child responds in faith, celebrate! You now have the opportunity to disciple your child to be more like Christ.

BUILD YOUR FAMILY LEGACY.

Dr. James Dobson leads you through his classic messages and new insights for today's families in these eight DVD-based Bible studies. Each Building a Family Legacy Bible study includes four-sessions with personal reflection and discussion guides along with a DVD of Dr. Dobson's teachings, introduced by his son, Ryan. Studies include:

Your Legacy Bible Study
Bringing Up Boys Bible Study
Bringing Up Girls Bible Study
Dare to Discipline Bible Study
The Strong-Willed Child Bible Study
Straight Talk to Men Bible Study
Love for a Lifetime Bible Study
Wanting to Believe Bible Study

Learn more at LifeWay.com/Legacy

DR. JAMES DOBSON BUILDING A FAMILY LEGACY™

Dr. James Dobson's **BUILDING A FAMILY LEGACY** campaign includes films, Bible studies, and books designed to help families of all ages and stages. Dr. Dobson's wisdom, insight, and humor promise to strengthen marriages and help parents meet the remarkable challenges of raising children. Most importantly, **BUILDING A FAMILY LEGACY** will inspire parents to lead their children to personal faith in Jesus Christ.

Learn more at

BUILDINGAFAMILYLEGACY.COM

BUILDING A FAMILY LEGACY BOOKS

From Dr. James Dobson and Tyndale Momentum

Bringing Up Boys • 978-1-4143-9133-5
Also available in hardcover (978-0-8423-5266-6) and audio CDs
(978-0-8423-2297-3)

Bringing Up Girls • 978-1-4143-9132-8
Also available in hardcover (978-1-4143-0127-3) and audio CDs
read by Dr. James Dobson (978-1-4143-3650-3)

The New Strong-Willed Child • 978-1-4143-9134-2
Also available in hardcover (978-0-8423-3622-2) and audio
CDs (978-0-8423-8799-6), as well as *The New Strong-Willed
Child Workbook* (978-1-4143-0382-6)

The New Dare to Discipline • 978-1-4143-9135-9

Straight Talk to Men • 978-1-4143-9131-1

AVAILABLE IN 2015

Love for a Lifetime
Revised and expanded edition
978-1-4964-0328-5